CONSULTATION
for
YOUTH GROUPS

Tips for Better Decision-Making

Joan Hernandez

PRAISE FOR *CONSULTATION FOR YOUTH GROUPS:*
Tips for Better Decision-Making
by Joan Hernandez

In clear, concise language, this book achieves both a conceptual understanding and a behavioral description of the basic principles of consultation. The author describes how different forms of leadership and the personal qualities of the group members contribute to or detract from an effective decision process. Although targeted to youth, it is also an excellent summary of collaborative decision making for people of any age. Engaging stories help to illustrate basic principles. Exercises and discussion questions make the book perfect for a workshop format.

Robert Giebitz, Phd. Organizational Learning & Learning Sciences

OTHER BOOKS BY
JOAN HERNANDEZ

Transformative Leadership: Developing the Hidden Dimension (co-author)

Transformative Leadership: Mastering the Hidden Dimension-Workbook (co-author)

Transformative Leadership for Youth: Practical and Fun Exercises to Build Self-Confidence and Resilience in a Crazy World

Strengthening the Capabilities of Giving Love and Encouragement

Unity in Diversity: The Role of Consultation

Transforming Relationships: Through Better Communication and Conflict Resolution

Love, Courtship and Marriage

Moral Leadership: An Introduction for Bahá'ís

The Baha'i Response to the Crisis of Our Time: What Each One of Us Can Do.

Joan Hernandez Author Page

Website: transformativeleadershipeducation.org

Newsletter: https://tinyurl.com/translead9

APPRECIATION

My deepest appreciation goes to Dr. Eloy Anello and other colleagues at Núr University who through their work in the fields of Transformative Leadership and Youth Leadership have contributed with their concepts and anecdotes to the understanding of consultation presented in this book.

Special thanks to Jessica Kerr for the cover design.

Joan Barstow Hernandez
Santa Cruz de la Sierra, Bolivia
transformativeleadershipeducation.org
translead9@gmail.com

CONTENTS

"No power can exist except through unity. No welfare and no well-being can be attained except through consultation." [1] Bahá'u'lláh

DOMINANT STYLES OF LEADERSHIP OBSTRUCT GROUP FUNCTIONING

Dominant styles of leadership, such as those exercised by authoritarian, paternalistic, know-it-all, or manipulative leaders, prevent the group from discovering its creative potential, because these types of leaders consider themselves superior to other members of the group.

First and foremost, they control the decision-making process. Although at times they may ask others to share their ideas, they rarely listen to those ideas attentively or take them into account when making the final decision. Rather, they impose their own ideas.

Secondly, they do not strive to facilitate the development of the capabilities of the group members. Rather, the members simply follow the orders of the leader, often realizing work of a routine nature. The leader is not interested in helping them to develop new capabilities.

Therefore, a requisite for group decision-making is the practice of moral leadership, and moral democracy, which recognizes the potential of the group to make better decisions and carry out more challenging tasks than any one person could do alone.

How Can We Serve?

In a student organization, the president asked the members to give their ideas for a service project that they could carry out in the community.

"We could clean up the neighborhood park, so that the little kids have a nice place to play," suggested one student.

"We could prepare skits and present them in other schools, to help the students reflect on the importance of moral values," suggested another.

"We could offer to tutor elementary school kids in subjects in which they have problems, such as math," proposed a third.

"Thanks for your ideas," said the president. "What we are going to do is: offer to clean up the playground every Friday.

Discussion Questions:

In this story, did the president consider the ideas of the other members? Was there true participation?

Have you participated in organizations in which the president or leader acted in this way? How did the members feel?

CONSULTATION REQUIRES DETACHMENT FROM PERSONAL INTERESTS

People have different ideas. They also have different interests and needs.

At times, in a group decision-making process, each member tries to influence the process so that the decisions made will benefit him or a certain group to which he belongs. For example, when his class was trying to decide where to have their end-of-the-year party, Mark stubbornly insisted that it be in a particular club, even though it was too expensive for everyone in the class to attend. What his classmates didn't know was that the club belonged to his uncle, and that he had promised to give a tip to Mark if the party was realized there.

When each person thinks only of himself and his own personal interests, he tends to use whatever means he can to achieve his ends. He tries to exert pressure on others so that they will give in to his desires. He resorts to personal attacks to discredit others and their motives. He presents half-truths that favor his own position and weaken the position of others. He forms coalitions with other members, promising to help them obtain certain interests of their own in the future, in exchange for their support.

Decisions resulting from pressure, negotiation or coalition-building are not characterized by justice, equity or concern for the well-being of all.

Consultation, on the other hand, is a method of decision-making based on an impartial search for truth by all members of the group, and characterized by an atmosphere of love and harmony. Its goal is making just decisions that benefit all, without excluding anyone or discriminating against any group. Therefore, productive consultation requires that each member conscientiously strive to detach himself from whatever personal interests he may have, focusing on the common good.

THE SHIPWRECK

Four men managed to survive a shipwreck and were in a lifeboat with only a small amount of food and water. They didn't know how long it might take in order for them to be picked up, but feared it might be weeks. One of them suggested that they act "democratically", and take a vote on what to do. The strongest three formed a coalition and decided to throw the weakest man overboard so that they would have a better chance to survive.

Discussion Questions:

Who benefits from decisions that are made as a result of conflicts between personal interests?

How does this method of decision-making affect the unity of the group?

Are you in agreement with the type of "democracy" that was practiced by the men in the boat? Why not?

CONSULTATION IS BASED ON THE INVESTIGATION OF TRUTH

The situations that we face in life are complex and can usually be interpreted in different ways. Therefore, it is impossible for any one person to have a complete grasp of all aspects of a particular situation. Rather, her understanding of truth will be influenced by her knowledge, her life experiences and also by her values and principles.

For example, a group of students may be consulting about the best way to study for an exam. However, each one may give a different suggestion. One may emphasize the importance of taking good notes in class. Another may say that what works for him is explaining to someone else what he has learned, making a verbal summary. A third may emphasize the value of using mental maps and other graphic organizers to diagram the relationships between different aspects of what he has studied. Still another may stress the importance of studying each day, rather than cramming the night before a test.

If each student thinks that she is the "sole owner" of the truth, and insists that her suggestion is the best, the group members will most likely end up fighting among themselves.

However, if they understand the purpose of consultation to be a broadening and deepening of their understanding, which they can only achieve through truly listening to one another, then they will make an effort to understand the "part of the truth" which each member perceives. This, in turn, facilitates coming to an agreement based on a shared understanding of the truth of the situation, an understanding constructed by the whole group, taking into account the ideas proposed by the different members.

Discussion Questions:

Why is it beneficial to try to achieve a fuller understanding of the truth of any situation before making a decision?

Once a person understands that she doesn't "own" the "whole truth" related to any particular situation, how does this influence her attitude towards ideas and opinions different from her own?

THE BLIND MEN AND THE ELEPHANT

Six blind men passed their days seated by the side of a road. Every day a herd of elephants came down the road. The blind men heard the people talking about the elephants, became curious, and began asking each other: "What kind of creature is an elephant?" Then one of the blind men had an idea.

"Tomorrow, when the elephants come by, we can stop the boy who cares for them and ask him to let us touch one of the elephants. That way we can experience for ourselves what an elephant really is."

The next day the blind men carried out their plan. But one of them was also crippled and could not walk, so he told the others: "I'll wait here. After you all touch the elephant, you can come back and tell me what it is like."

The first blind man touched the trunk of the elephant and exclaimed: "Now I know what an elephant is like! It's like a snake!"

The second blind man touched the leg of the elephant and shouted. "I've got it! An elephant is like a tree trunk!"

The third blind man touched the side of the elephant, stretching his arms to each side as far as he could. "An elephant is like a wall," was his conclusion.

The fourth blind man grabbed the tail of the elephant, and exclaimed: "An elephant is like a rope!"

And the fifth blind man touched one of the gigantic tusks of the elephant and screamed: "Now I know! An elephant is like a pickax!"

The five blind men returned and began telling their friend about the elephant.

"It's like a snake."

"What are you saying? It's not like a snake at all! It's like a tree trunk!"

"No! It's like a wall!"

"You're all crazy! It's like a rope!"

"What's wrong with you? Didn't you feel that it's like a pickax?"

The five blind men began to argue among themselves. Each one insisted that he was right and made fun of the ideas of his companions. They continued arguing until they became very angry at one another.

Finally, the sixth blind man told them: "If you continue like this, I don't think we'll ever understand what an elephant is really like. We will only be able to discover the truth of the matter, if we practice consultation. Let's listen to the ideas of each person, one at a time, and try to understand what he perceived about the elephant and why he thinks that way. Then, once we understand the different points of view, together we can construct a more complete understanding of the truth.

Discussion Questions:

What does this story teach us about the investigation of truth?

What does it teach us about consultation?

CONSULTATION CONSIDERS
THE WELL-BEING OF EVERYONE

"Consultation is the operating expression of justice in human affairs."[2] Prosperity of Humankind

Achieving a fuller understanding of truth is only the first step in consultation. Then, we need to use that understanding to make just, equitable decisions, striving to make the wisest decision possible within the options available.

If we keep in mind the following principle, it can help us in our efforts to make just decisions:

The well-being of the whole depends on the well-being of each of its members; conversely, the well-being of the members depends on the well-being of the whole.

Therefore, when striving to make a just decision, we can ask ourselves: What brings the greatest benefit to the group as a whole, without leaving out or harming any member of our group or of any other group in our school, in our community, in our region, in our country, or in the world?

Then, we can search for the best possible balance between the well-being of the whole and the well-being of each member and/or group.

THE COOPERATIVE STUDENT

There were two students in a school, who always got the highest grades in their class.

One of the students was extremely self-centered. He kept to himself and never shared his notes with his fellow students, nor helped them to study for tests, because he was afraid that if he did, one of them might get better grades than he did.

The other student was very cooperative. She always took time to help her classmates and to explain what they hadn't understood in class, illustrating her explanations with practical examples and working with them until they were able to resolve on their own whatever had been giving them trouble.

Month after month, the cooperative student had the best grades in the class, and her self-centered companion came in second.

When asked: "Why do you think that you always get the best grades?", she answered: "It's because I always help my companions. When I explain something to them, I understand it better. Explaining, I consolidate my own knowledge to such a degree that I never forget."

Discussion Questions:

Think of a practical example in which the well-being of the whole contributes to the well-being of each member of a group (class, school, neighborhood, community).

Dramatize the example.

GUIDELINES THAT LEAD TO
PRODUCTIVE CONSULTATION

Even when we know that the purpose of consultation is to investigate the truth in order to make just decisions, at times the way we act in a meeting obstructs productive consultation.

Some of us have the habit of talking too much. We are so full of enthusiasm for our own ideas, and we talk so much, that we deprive others of the opportunity to participate.

Others are quiet and timid. Since we are not sure if our ideas are good or not, we prefer not to share them. As a consequence, we deprive others of the "part of the truth" that perhaps only we have perceived.

Others are a bit aggressive. If someone proposes an idea that is not compatible with what we have suggested, we immediately respond, attacking the other person and his suggestion and defending what we have said

Still others get distracted during consultation. We don't pay much attention to the topic of the consultation and then we say things that don't relate directly with that subject. Or we make jokes or tell stories that don't help move the consultation towards a decision.

Others simply try to please. We listen to what one of our friends say and then we support their point of view out of friendship, rather than analyzing the ideas involved.

To avoid these and other problems that frequently occur when a group of people tries to consult, we need to practice certain guidelines during the consultation. These include:

- Promoting unity and harmony among the members.
- Sharing what our conscience dictates,
- Combining truthfulness and courtesy when speaking,
- Showing appreciation for a diversity of ideas,
- Supporting the decisions made.

Discussion Question:

Consider each problem mentioned on the previous page, one at a time. Try to identify rules or guidelines that the group could adopt, which would help to solve each problem, contributing to more harmonious, productive consultation.

UNITY IS THE FOUNDATION

It is impossible to have productive consultation if there is not a spirit of unity and harmony among the participants.

If there are feelings of hostility, estrangement, or anger among some of the participants, these negative feelings will prevent them from understanding one another's viewpoints. Rather, each will tend to reject or criticize everything said by the person towards whom she has negative feelings.

Outside the meeting, those who have the problem should try to resolve it, and each one should make an effort to transform her negative feelings into positive ones. Then they can consult.

However, unity consists in much more than the absence of negative feelings. It implies the existence of feelings of affection, respect and appreciation among the members.

This condition can be better achieved when the members of a group or organization cultivate friendly relationships, not only in their meetings, but also in their daily lives, showing interest in one another's well-being and helping each other in the problems of daily life.

In the meetings some practices that help strengthen unity and harmony include:

--At the beginning of each meeting turn towards God, asking Him to illumine the group so that it may make decisions that truly benefit all.

-- Always speak with courtesy and respect.

-- Listen to others' ideas with attention, interest and respect.

Discussion Questions:

Describe what generally happens in a meeting in which there is a lack of unity among the participants.

Make a list of concrete actions that each member of your group or organization can do in order to become more united.

18

SHARE WHAT YOUR CONSCIENCE DICTATES

Since consultation is based on the investigation of truth, when consulting, each of us needs to share what we sincerely think.

For that reason, even those of us, who by nature are shy and prefer to listen, should make an effort to share our opinions, especially when we realize that we have ideas, which have not been expressed by anyone else.

At times we have an opinion that is very different from, or even opposed to, the opinions of everyone else. The others may have given their ideas first, and everyone seems to be in agreement. In such a situation, it is easy to remain quiet, and not bring up an idea that will disturb the consensus. If fact, it is easy to justify doing just that, as a means of maintaining unity.

But this attitude does not contribute to deepening the understanding of the truth of the situation. Therefore, we need to have the courage to say what we think, even when no one else thinks that way. If the other members of the group are truly searching for truth, at times the idea of just one person can change the way the whole group sees a situation.

THE CHAMPIONSHIP

In the 10th grade class meeting, the physical education teacher informed the students that he was organizing a soccer championship that would begin in two weeks. All the students were enthusiastic and thanked the teacher, except for one, who remained quiet, thinking.

Finally, he pulled together his courage and said: "I am as happy as my classmates about the championship, but I was wondering if it wouldn't be better to postpone it until one week later. In exactly 2 ½ weeks we have a math exam, and not only has the math teacher warned us that it is going to be hard, it is also going to be our main grade in math this quarter. If we are in the middle of the championship, no one will study."

At first, all the students remained quiet, surprised that their classmate had dared to suggest a change in the plans of the teacher. But then they saw the wisdom of his suggestion and supported it.

The teacher changed the dates of the championship, which was a great success! Moreover, the students decided to help each other prepare for the math exam, and almost everyone got a good grade on that too. And all because one student had the courage to say what he really thought.

Discussion Questions:

Why is it often difficult to give an opinion that is different from the ideas of others?

Why is it important to share what our conscience dictates?

COMBINE TRUTHFULNESS AND COURTESY

"Truthfulness is the foundation of all the virtues of the world of humanity."[3] 'Abdu'l-Bahá

"Courtesy, ... is the prince of virtues."[4] Bahá'u'lláh

Narrator: Consultation is more effective when everyone practices both truthfulness and courtesy.

Youth 1: Why is truthfulness important in consultation?

Youth 2: If each of us does not share the truth as he or she sees it, consultation cannot achieve its purpose, which is the investigation of truth. Moreover, a lack of truthfulness and sincerity between people causes mistrust and destroys relationships.

Youth 1: And why is courtesy important?

Youth 2: Courtesy is extremely important in establishing unity. Telling the truth without courtesy can hurt people and also destroy relationships.

Youth 1: At times it is difficult to be both truthful and courteous at the same time. Some people and cultures emphasize truthfulness at the expense of courtesy. Others emphasize courtesy at the expense of truthfulness.

Youth 2: That's why we all need to evaluate our practice of these two qualities, and make an effort to further develop them, putting special emphasis on whichever quality is weaker.

By no means does this imply being half truthful and half courteous, only telling "white lies", for example. Rather, it implies that we develop each of these qualities to the highest degree to which we are capable, and then let them balance out each other.

Youth 1: Now I understand. In this way we can learn to be simultaneously both truthful and courteous.

Discussion Question:

In pairs, write a paragraph in which you explain why truthfulness is the foundation of other virtues.

Activity:

Role-play situations in which it is necessary to say something difficult to someone else. Practice saying it with both truthfulness and courtesy.

SHOW APPRECIATION FOR A DIVERSITY OF IDEAS

Good consultation leads to better decisions than those made by one person alone. But this only happens, when through consultation, the members develop a broader, more complete understanding of the truth than that which each one had originally.

This implies that we should not only tolerate ideas that are different from our own; rather we should welcome them, because they give us the opportunity to understand aspects of the truth that we had not previously considered. .

The conflict of ideas is very different from a clash of personalities. It implies the practice of "unity in diversity"; that is, having cordial relationships with others, while respecting, showing interest in and trying to learn from their ideas. In practical terms, this implies:

- Not insisting obstinately on our own ideas. If others don't respond to them, we have to learn to practice detachment.
- Never making fun of another person or disdaining what she says, but rather making an effort to understand the part of the truth she is perceiving;
- Not getting angry if others propose ideas that are different or contrary to our own;
- Always treating others with courtesy, cordiality and respect.

WHAT WOULD YOU DO?

1) *John is convinced that the best place to celebrate the class party is at his house. He has suggested it a number of times, explaining the advantages of having it there, but everyone seems to be in agreement with having it at Edward's house.*

¿What should John do?

2) *The class is consulting about their plans for celebrating Mothers' Day. Suddenly, Louise, who is very timid and hardly ever participates, raises her hand and suggests: "Let's make cards for our mothers. We could draw a picture and write 'Happy Mother's Day.'" "What a childish idea!" laughed Ralph. "Only little kids in first grade do things like that. We have to do something much better."*

What guidelines of consultation did Ralph forget? How do you think that Louise felt? Do you think she will participate again?

3) *A group of classmates was consulting about how to present an exposition for their science class. "You guys prepare the written part," suggested Mary, "and I'll be in charge of the oral presentation." "I don't think that would be just," responded Joe. "The written part is more difficult. I think it would be better for each of us to prepare part of the written report and then explain that part in the oral presentation." "Are you calling me lazy?" Mary shouted at him. "I only want the project to be a success, and I know that I give better oral presentations than the rest of you do. If you want to do it that way, it doesn't matter to me. But don't blame me if we get a bad grade." Then Mary got up and left the room.*

What guidelines of consultation did Mary forget?

SUPPORT THE DECISIONS MADE

Unity is the foundation of consultation. It needs to be cultivated before, during and after consultation.

Even though the ideal in consultation is to reach consensus and make decisions with which everyone agrees, when it is not possible to resolve a difference in opinion, at times it is necessary to take a vote and accept the decision of the majority.

In that case, it is extremely important that those who were not in agreement with the decision support it and help in its execution, without criticism. If they do, unity will be maintained.

Then, if the decision really is mistaken, in time everyone will realize it and together will be able to modify or change the decision. On the contrary, if the members who were not in agreement with the decision complain about it and do not support it, and then it fails, that will be the cause of even greater disunity.

Those who were against the decision will boast that they were right. And those who were in agreement with the decision will complain that the failure was caused by the criticisms and lack of support of the others.

The truth will never be known. And the disunity provoked will hinder the group from agreeing on and carrying out other projects.

"Though one of the parties may be in the right and they disagree that will be the cause of a thousand wrongs, but if they agree and both parties are in the wrong, as it is in unity the truth will be revealed and the wrong made right."[5]   'Abdu'l-Bahá

25

THE CLASS PROJECT

The class had decided on the project of painting the wall around the school with murals promoting the Rights of Children and Youth. As a first step they needed to raise $50 with which to buy paints, paintbrushes and other materials. During the consultation Mary had suggested that they organize a raffle to raise the money, but her classmates insisted that a dance would be better, so that they could have fun and raise money at the same time. Mary tried to explain that the expenses involved in organizing the dance would be much greater and that the profits would not be as sure. But when her classmates insisted, she accepted the decision and was the first to help in the organization. Everyone worked hard, printing up the invitations, checking out different bands, and making the decorations.

The night of the dance, unfortunately it rained and very few youth came to the dance. At the end of the evening when they finally had time to calculate the expenses and the proceeds, at first they thought that they had lost money. But when they finally finished calculating everything, they had made a profit of $10. Mary felt like saying "I told you so!" but she restrained herself and only asked: "Now what shall we do?"

After consulting about a variety of ideas, they decided to use the $10 to buy something to raffle, and to distribute the sale of the tickets among themselves in such a way that they would be sure to make $70.

Discussion Questions:

If some members of a group criticize a decision with which they are not in agreement, do not support it, and in truth, the decision does not lead to good results, what often happens?

If a decision is mistaken, but the whole group works in unity to implement it, in time what often happens?

What should you do if the group makes a decision with which you are not in agreement? Why?

PERSONAL QUALITIES THAT CONTRIBUTE TO GOOD CONSULTATION

In order to practice the guidelines of consultation appropriately, we need to develop and practice certain qualities in our lives. These qualities, which contribute to good consultation, are:

Purity of Intention: Be sincere. Never try to manipulate the consultation in benefit of our own personal interests.

Radiance of Spirit: Be positive. Smile. See the positive side of each idea. Radiate happiness, optimism and enthusiasm.

Detachment: Don't cling obstinately to our own ideas. Once we have contributed an idea to the consultation, assume that the idea now belongs to the group. Don't get upset if others propose changes, or suggest opposing ideas.

Attraction to Transcendent Values: Love God and humanity. Be committed to the practice of qualities, such as justice, unity, truthfulness, and courtesy.

Humility and Modesty: Do not consider ourselves to be superior to others. Do not boast or try to put ourselves above others.

Patience in Difficulties: If it is difficult to make a decision, remain calm, without getting irritated or complaining about others. Also avoid accepting an inadequate decision, just in order to end the meeting quickly. Calmly persevere.

Spirit of Service: Be cooperative. Be sensitive to the needs of others and respond to them. Help others to develop their capabilities and to learn new skills.

Discussion Questions:

Give examples of how each quality helps to better consultation.

In groups, prepare dramatizations that show what happens when the members do not practice one of these qualities. The other groups should try to identify the quality or qualities that are not being adequately practiced.

SELF-EVALUATION

Which of these practices DO NOT help to foster unity?

_____ Speaking with courtesy and respect.

_____ Saying what you think of the other person with complete frankness, -even though it hurts.

_____ Listening to the ideas of others with interest and attention, even when they are boring.

_____Participating in social get-togethers outside of meetings.

If the whole group has given similar ideas and you have an idea which is completely different, you should:

_____ Remain silent in order to maintain group unity.

_____ Share your idea courteously and accept whatever response comes from the others.

_____ Tell the rest of the group that they are mistaken.

_____ Wait until after the meeting and share your idea with a friend.

If John invites Tom to a party, and Tom knows that he will not be able to attend because of an activity with his girlfriend's family, which of the following responses best combines truthfulness and courtesy?

_____ "Of course, I'll be there."

_____ "I have better things to do that day. My girl comes first!"

_____ "I'd like to go, but I have already made a prior commitment to be with my girlfriend's family that day. I hope you'll invite me again on another occasion."

_____ "I'm sorry, but I don't like parties."

28

After consulting about what murals to paint on the walls of the school, Mark proposes that they paint landscapes. Which of the following replies best shows a conflict of ideas and not of personalities?

_____ Why do you want to paint landscapes? How boring!

_____ What a stupid idea! No one but you would come up with an idea like that!

_____ Landscapes??!! You're crazy! We should take advantage of the opportunity to paint something that communicates a message—something related to drugs, the environment, or peace.

_____ That's a possibility. But what about painting something that communicates a message; for example, something related to drugs or the environment?

What should you do when you are not in agreement with a decision made by the majority?

_____ Accept it and support it, showing good will and enthusiasm as you help carry it out.

_____ Accept it, but don't get involved, leaving those who supported the decision to carry it out.

_____Accept it in front of the group, but criticize it outside the meeting.

_____Tell everyone that a mistake has been made, and that they should not get involved.

STEPS IN DECISION-MAKING

A GIFT FOR OUR TEACHER

All the students in the high school liked Mr. Smith's classes. He made it easy to understand mathematics. So, as Teachers' Day drew near, students from different classes were consulting about what they could give him.

In class A, each student had a different idea based on his own opinion. The ideas were diverse, but at last the group decided to give him an expensive perfume. They also decided that each one of the 25 students should contribute $1, and they named a commission to buy the perfume. But when the commission went to buy the perfume, the members discovered that it cost more than $25. So they decided to buy a shirt, guessing at the proper size.

In class B, the students began by consulting about what they thought Mr. Smith would like, taking into account comments that he himself had made in class. Some students who had visited the teacher at his home commented that they had observed that he liked handicrafts. Another commented that he had observed that the billfold of the teacher was getting old. Combining these facts, the students decided to find out how much it would cost to buy an engraved leather billfold. The commission in charge reported back that the billfold would cost $10, so each student would have to contribute $0.40.

On Teachers' Day, each class gave their present to Mr. Smith....

Discussion Questions:

Which gift do you think that the teacher liked best? Why?

What differences did you observe in the way that the students in the two groups decided on the gift to buy?

Why is it important to investigate the facts before making a decision?

Activity: Finish the story, making it clear why it is important to investigate the facts before making a decision.

Since consultation is based on the investigation of truth, before making any decision, we need to investigate the facts. If we do not do so, it is easy to make a wrong decision.

For example, if a class is consulting about where to go for an outing, it is important to investigate the cost of the transportation to the different possible destinations, and the time that the trip will take. Without these facts, a decision may be made that seems good at the moment, but turns out to be impractical to carry out.

Likewise, when a problem comes up between two or more people, it is important to investigate the facts as perceived from different points of view, before making a decision. If this is not done, the decision may be unjust.

Consultation will be more productive if the topic is well-defined and then four steps are followed in the decision-making process. The first two steps contribute to the process of the investigation of truth. The other two focus on the identification of alternatives for action and then on the process of choosing between them

0) Delimit the topic to keep the consultation focused.

Often when we begin to consult, many related ideas come up. This impedes decision-making because each person is pursuing a different line of thought. For example, when consulting about a school outing, some students may give ideas about where to go, while others give suggestions for the program. If this occurs, the coordinator can delimit the topic by suggesting: "First, let's define the program. Then we can consult about where to go."

Before even beginning to consult, we can identify a specific topic, or a list of topics. If other issues come up, we add them to the list and come back to them later.

Formulating a clear vision of the desired results coherent with our principles also helps keep us on track. In the case of the school outing, the vision might be: "affordable fun in which all can participate." A vision helps us to make decisions that lead to the desired outcomes.

Without clarity of vision, we can expend effort on ideas that seemingly go in the right direction, but that ultimately do not lead to what we desire. For example, time could be spent consulting on the activities that could be realized in a particular place that is so expensive that not all of the students could participate.

1) *Investigate the facts.*

Depending on the topic, we can do this rapidly or go into considerable depth.

- At times the facts are obvious and can be listed quickly.
- At others, we discover that we do not know all the relevant facts and need to identify areas that need further investigation before proceeding.

Investigating the facts is part of the process of investigating truth. It is almost impossible to make just decisions without full, correct information. When consulting about matters that involve a number of people or groups in the community, it is especially important to find out what everyone thinks about the matter, and not base the decision on information provided by only one party.

2) *Identify the relevant principles.*

"There are spiritual principles, or what some call human values, by which solutions can be found for every social problem." [6] The Promise of World Peace

Just, lasting solutions are coherent with principles. Therefore, the identification of relevant principles is an essential part of the investigation of truth. We use the word "principles' to refer to both:

a) spiritual qualities, such as justice, unity, honesty and truthfulness; and

b) social principles, such as:

the elimination of all kinds of prejudice, whether these be racial, religious, national, regional or of social class;

the equality of rights and opportunities for men and women;

32

universal education, which implies both the right of all to education, as well as a universal outlook in what is taught;

the elimination of extremes of riches and poverty;

a balance between intellectual knowledge and spiritual development;

a recognition of justice as the source of unity, and of unity as the source of power for human progress.

Analysis of a Situation:

The girls in the class are mad because they want to play basketball, but the boys are using the court and don't give them a chance.

¿What principles should the class take into account when they consult on what to do about this problem?

What facts might be necessary to know or find out? How could the class go about finding out these facts?

SUGGEST A VARIETY OF ALTERNATIVE SOLUTIONS

At times consultation bogs down, because the participants begin to debate the advantages and disadvantages of the first "solution" suggested, dividing into two groups, those in favor of it and those against it. In the ensuing debate, other ideas, which may be even better, are not even brought up.

One way to avoid problems of this type is to initiate the consultation by asking each person to give his own idea, without commenting on the ideas suggested by others. This gives the opportunity to timid members of the group to share their ideas.

So that all ideas are taken into account, someone can write each suggestion on a white board or large paper where all can see it. Once we have a sizeable list of proposals, we can begin analyzing the suggestions, discarding some, accepting others and considering how to better ideas that have potential but need modification.

We can also see how ideas relate and how we could take into account valid aspects of more than one idea, gradually coming to a decision that is often a new creation, distinct from any of the original ideas.

Before adopting a proposed solution, we should take time to evaluate it to make sure that it:
- takes into account relevant principles;
- leads to the desired outcome;
- does not demand an unreasonable amount of human or material resources.

Activity: Using the form on the following page, formulate a project of something your class can do to better your school. In the process, practice everything you have learned about consultation.

After filling out the form, answer the following questions:

In what facts did you base your decision to do this project?

What principles did you take into account?

PROJECT:			
ACTIVITIES	People in charge	Materials	Dates

LEAVE A REVIEW

If you liked the book, I need you to leave a review on Amazon. This will enable more people to learn about the book and use it to work with youth in their communities

USING THIS BOOK WITH GROUPS OF YOUTH

Consultation for Youth Groups is designed to use with groups of youth who participate in the group discussions and carry out the suggested activities together.

Now that you are familiar with the contents of the book, think of a group of youth with whom you can apply it. If they are part of an organization that already exists, such as scouts, a church group, a recreational center, or any other organization where youth congregate, you can approach the person in charge, share the contents of the book, and consult about the possibility of incorporating the contents of the book into the program.

Another option is to offer the course as an extra-curricular activity in a school, or simply organize a group with youth from your neighborhood.

When using the book with a group of youth, it is preferable that each one have their own copy. You can order both print and digital copies on Amazon at http://tinyurl.com/youthconsult .

OTHER BOOKS TO STUDY WITH YOUTH

If you found the present book useful and you have not yet read *Transformative Leadership for Youth*, you will probably want to.

Effective consultation, which was the topic of this book, is only one of 18 capabilities explored in *Transformative Leadership for Youth*, which is designed as a workbook to help youth respond to the many social challenges they face in today's world.

By focusing on both personal transformation and social action, and by discussing with their peers what they are learning, youth develop new capabilities and confidence in themselves

Leadership vs. Being a Leader

Often leadership is considered to be the exclusive calling of a few. *Transformative Leadership for Youth* examines how to exercise leadership without being in a position of authority or having a formal position as the head of a group. It shows youth how they can exercise leadership
- at home,
- at school
- in teams, clubs and the organizations to which they belong.

Through participating in the readings and activities in *Transformative Leadership,* both you and the youth will internalize a conceptual framework of leadership consisting of six elements:

1. A spirit of service
2. The purpose of leadership: personal and social transformation
3. The fundamental moral responsibility: the investigation and application of truth
4. A conviction of the essential nobility of human beings
5. Transcendence
6. The development of capabilities

By consulting on the elements and 18 capabilities of Transformative Leadership and carrying out exercises to apply them, youth discover solutions to common problems they face in their lives, such as bullying behaviors.

In the process they acquire the concepts and capabilities they need to better direct their own lives and to contribute to an ever-progressing civilization, empowering them to exercise leadership wherever they find themselves.

Faced with the tremendous challenges that characterize this stage of human history, Transformative Leadership gives youth an idea of what they can do to build a better world –- starting wherever they are.

Drawing on her experience of over 25 years working with teachers, parents and youth, Joan Hernandez has developed a workbook that truly empowers youth and motivates their transformation.

You can purchase it at https://tinyurl.com/TransLidYouth

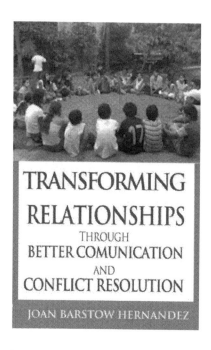

Transforming Relationships through Better Communication and Conflict Resolution

Who has not suffered from communication problems?

How often we explain something clearly, and yet the other person acts as if he had not heard a word we said. Or with the best of intentions we want to clarify a point, and the other reacts as if we were attacking him or her.

Knowing how to communicate clearly and how to ensure that what we have said has been understood by the other person are some of the many skills learned BY reading this book and carrying out the activities it suggests.

In addition to clarifying communication skills, the text also explores the process of conflict resolution, presenting six principles underlying the collaborative mode of resolving conflicts, which allows everyone to win.

By implementing these principles, you can improve the way you handle conflicts when they arise.

So that you can help others with their conflicts, the book also explains the four main steps in mediating conflicts.

The language of the text is simple and easy to understand, including numerous anecdotes and examples to illustrate the explanations.

Each topic is further complemented by a discussion question or activity that helps consolidate learning.

<u>Love Courtship and Marriage</u>

Do you want to prepare yourself for a **wonderful marriage**?

This book offers guidance from the Bahá'í Writings for all those of any age who are interested in developing a good marriage, based on the assumption that **marital success depends on the moral and spiritual qualities of both partners.**

The chapters not only explore some of these qualities, but also give practical suggestion on getting to **know the character of one another** before marriage, practices that **strengthen the marriage** and how to **face the tests** that are an inevitable part of any marriage.

Comments by Readers:

"The book is great. Whenever people here read it, they say things like, "I wish I read this before I got married", or "Had I read this before I never would have gotten divorced."

Curt Porter. Guatemala

ABOUT THE AUTHOR

Joan Hernandez was born and grew up in the United States. Immediately after graduating from college, she moved to Guatemala to participate in voluntary service activities. In 1990 she moved to Bolivia, where she began her work with Núr University.

She began writing in the 1980's, but her work intensified at Núr, where she became known for her clear, practical, easily-understood style.

She has authored or co-authored more than twenty books in Spanish, and an increasing number in English, related to education, family relations, leadership, socio-economic development and the Baha'i Faith.

During 25 years she has also facilitated workshops at Núr University and throughout Latin America, as well as in the United States, Canada, Europe, and Africa. She also offers online courses.

She can be reached at **traslead9@gmail.com** o **juanitah48@gmail.com**

REFERENCES

[1] Bahá'u'lláh in *Consultation: A Compilation*, 1.2.

[2] Baha'i International Community. *Prosperity of Humankind*, Section III.

[3] 'Abdu'l-Bahá. *Tablets of 'Abdu'l-Bahá*, p. 459.

[4] Bahá'u'lláh. *Tablets of Bahá'u'lláh*. p. 88.

[5] 'Abdu'l-Bahá, quoted in *Principles of Bahá'í Administration*, p. 48.

[6] Universal House of Justice. *The Promise of World Peace*, Section II..

Made in United States
Orlando, FL
07 September 2022